SUNBIRD
PENGUIN

Published by Ladybird Books Ltd 2012
A Penguin Company
Penguin Books Ltd, 80 Strand, London, WC2R ORL, UK
Penguin Books Australia Ltd, Camberwell, Victoria, Australia
Penguin Group (NZ), 67 Apollo Drive, Rosedale, North Shore
0632, New Zealand (a division of Pearson New Zealand Ltd)
Sunbird is a trademark of Ladybird Books Ltd

Written by Virginia Blackburn
With thanks to models Jessica Gardner and Philippa McMaster
Model photography – Kitty Walker
Stylist – Rose Gardner
Cakes created by Isla Game

www.ladybird.com
ISBN: 978-1-40939-177-7
Printed in Italy

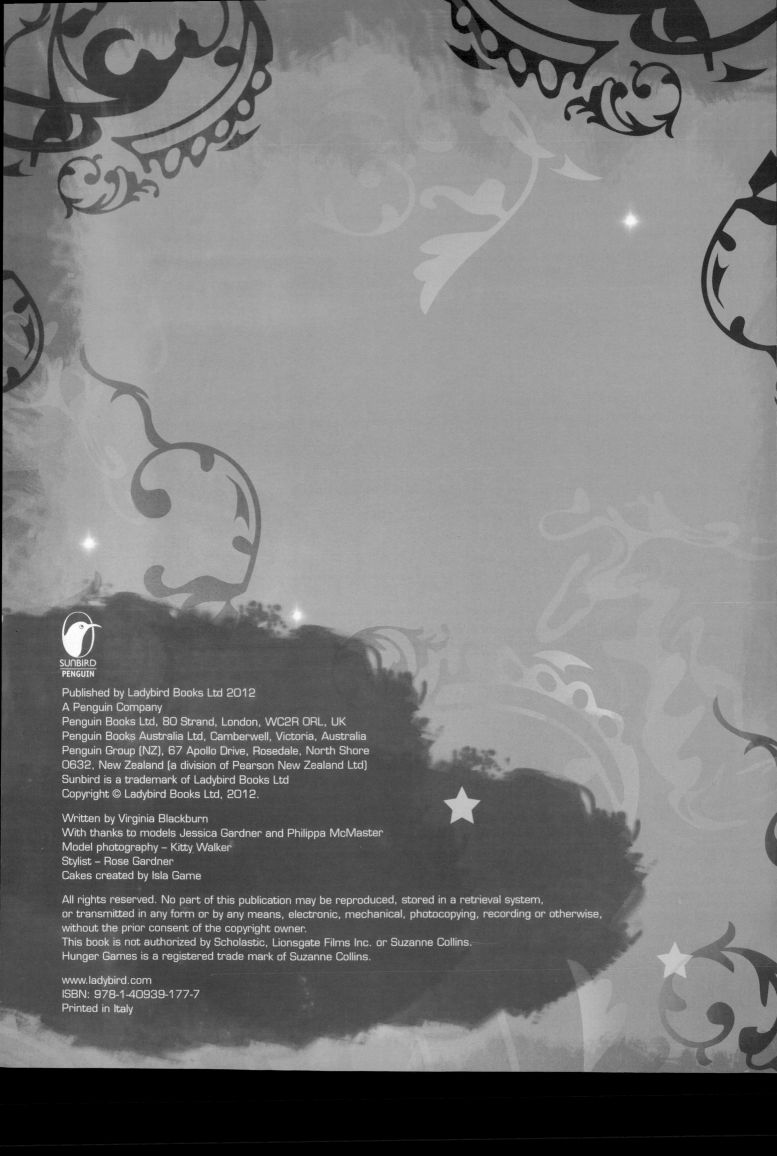

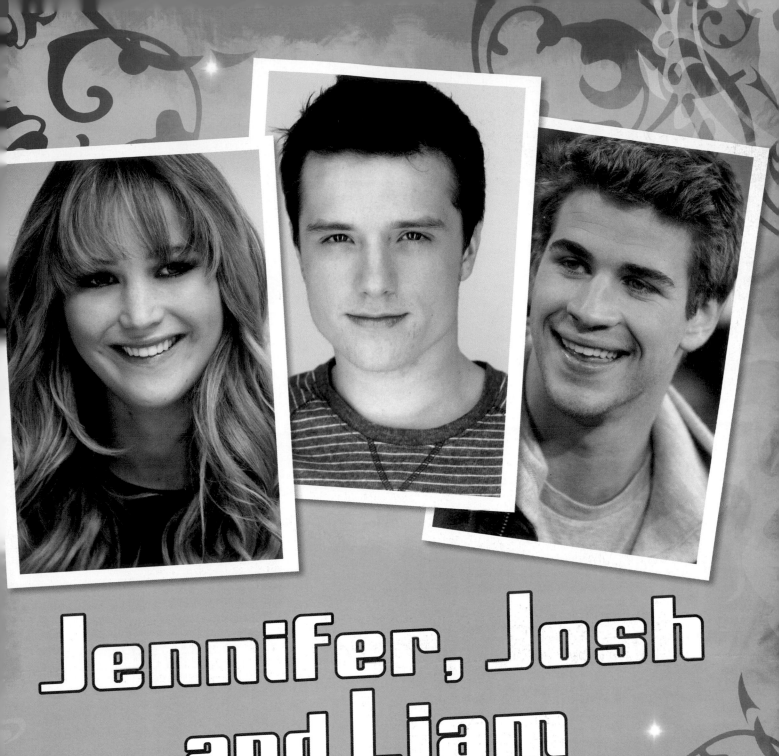

Jennifer, Josh and Liam

THE UNAUTHORIZED ANNUAL 2013

What's Inside?

Style Guide

Quizzes, Facts & Fun

Welcome to . . .

Stars of *The Hunger Games*

The Hunger Games is a sensation! It has a fan base that stretches across the entire globe. And we can't get enough of the supercool stars of the new film who struggle against the terrible rulers of the post-apocalyptic society of Panem. Jennifer Lawrence, Josh Hutcherson and Liam Hemsworth are the hottest trio on the planet right now.

So we've brought together everything you need to know about Jennifer, Josh and Liam in one handy place.

But that's only the start. We all want to look like Jennifer, right? So here you can find out how to recreate Jennifer's look or Katniss's style – with tips about clothes and make-up that can make you as gorgeous as Jennifer herself.

And you think you know about The Games? Here you'll find out everything you need to know about surviving in the wilderness, alongside super-fun quizzes to test your knowledge about our stars. Oh, and did you know the story is actually based on a Greek myth? Read on! You'll find out everything you need to know.

Jennifer Lawrence

Name: Jennifer Shrader Lawrence
Birthday: 15th August 1990
Starsign: Leo
Height: 5'7"
Hometown: Louisville, Kentucky

A Kentucky Girl

In the Beginning

Jennifer hails from Louisville, Kentucky, on the border of the Deep South and the Mid West, a "surprise" child after the birth of her two older brothers, Ben and Blaine. It was a very happy upbringing, which gave her a rock solid confidence that was to serve her very well as her career took off. According to Jennifer, her brothers used to fight each other over which one would get to fight her; once they even smeared peanut butter on her face and locked her in the basement with the family's three dachshunds who licked it all off! Her father, Gary, once owned a construction firm called Lawrence & Associates, while her mother Karen runs a children's camp in Oldham County.

Star Student

Jennifer studied at Kammerer Middle School, where she was expected to go on to Ballard High School. In her spare time she took part in church plays as well as spending a semester at the Walden Theatre. Jennifer was also a keen gymnast and thought that when she was older she might become a doctor. But fate had other ideas . . .

When Jennifer was fourteen, she went to New York for a short break with her family. They were watching the dancers at Union Square when a model scout approached and asked if he could take Jennifer's photo. Fortunately, her parents agreed, and the man took both Jennifer's picture and her mum's phone number. Soon afterwards, a modelling agency got in touch. Jennifer's career was on its way.

Did you know?

In her first school photo, Jennifer wore a green tuxedo and a red plaid tie which she wouldn't take off!

Start Spreading the News

Despite the fact that she was still so young, Jennifer's parents realised that a huge opportunity had opened up for her and they were keen to make the most of it. So Jennifer and her mother moved to New York. However, to everyone's surprise, it was not just as a model that Jennifer began to make it, but as an actress. Jennifer later told the *Globe and Mail* that her parents were the very opposite of stage parents and did all they could to stop it from happening. But it was going to happen anyway. 'I was like, "Thanks for raising me, but I'm going to take it from here." '

Did you know?

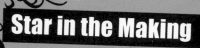

Jennifer was a real tomboy when she was growing up.

Star in the Making

And she did. The dabbling in acting she did when younger stood her in good stead – she started going to auditions and managed to get bit parts in *Medium*, *Cold Case*, *The Devil You Know* and *Monk*, before being signed up for *The Bill Engvall Show*. She spent three seasons with the show before it was cancelled. Jennifer was still only fifteen. In the meantime there was also modelling for Abercrombie & Fitch and a Burger King advert. She was beginning to make waves.

Fanatical about Film

In fact, for such a young actress, Jennifer was remarkably determined about what happened next. She'd been approached to do a series for Disney, but she decided that she wasn't a very Disney girl and so turned it down. Instead, although all her roles to date had been on television, it was films she wanted to do. Ironically, given that *The Hunger Games* was going to overtake it as the Next Big Thing, she auditioned for the *Twilight* saga, reading for the roles of Bella and Rosalie, but she was turned down.

In the Movies

Independent Girl

Initially, it seemed as if her career was going to be in small, independent films, her first was in the role of Tiff in 2008's *Garden Party*. She was pretty modest about that early work, however. She admits that at fifteen and sixteen she sucked, because she didn't know what she was doing, but told the *Globe and Mail*, 'Then I slowly stopped sucking.' She knows she's not immune from failure, but says 'I'm a hard worker, and when I set my mind to something, it usually happens.'

> **"When I set my mind to something, it usually happens"**

That same year it became apparent that Jennifer was not just another run-of-the-mill pretty girl. She took the role of Mariana in *The Burning Plain*, in which she starred alongside Charlize Theron and Kim Basinger. The film only achieved a limited release, but Jennifer certainly made an impact. She won an award for Best Young Emerging Actor at the Venice Film Festival.

Did you know?

In her spare time, Jennifer likes to paint and knit!

Eager Beaver

It wasn't long before Jennifer began attracting more attention. Later in 2008, she starred as Agnes, a young victim of abuse, in *The Poker House*. During 2009, she appeared in the music video 'The Mess I Made' from Parachute's album *Losing Sleep*, as well as in Jodie Foster's film *The Beaver*, starring the increasingly-controversial Mel Gibson. The reviews weren't great, but that didn't matter as far as Jennifer was concerned, she had already proved her mettle and was lining up plenty more work, too.

The Breakthrough

But it wasn't until the following year, in 2010, that Jennifer had her real breakthrough. Debra Granik cast her in *Winter's Bone* as seventeen-year-old Ree Dolly, who is forced to look after her mentally ill mother and younger brother and sister. After her father disappears whilst on bail for a drug dealing charge, Ree must set out into the dangerous world of drug dealing in order to find out what happened to her father, to protect her siblings and keep the family home.

Rave Reviews

A feel-good film it wasn't, but Jennifer caused a sensation. Reviews of both her and the film were almost universally positive. 'The movie would be unimaginable with anyone less charismatic playing Ree,' said *The New Yorker*. She was nominated for Best Actress at the Oscars, the second youngest person ever to be nominated in that category after Keisha Castle-Hughes in *Whale Rider*. But at just twenty years old, Jennifer felt she was very young for an Oscar nomination, telling *Louisville Magazine* 'I can, like, make a dentist appointment, barely. I don't even know how to shop online.'

Did you know?

For her role in *Winter's Bone*, she had to learn to chop wood, handle firearms and skin squirrels!

Staying Sane

Jennifer remained relatively unaffected by her increasing fame. Interviewers who met her around that time often commented on her air of confidence. She was overwhelmed neither by her success, nor the darkness she was so often called upon to examine in her movies. As she explained to one newspaper, 'So many people, after they've seen my movies, expect me to be intense and dark, and I'm not at all.' She has said that she avoids becoming emotionally drained by her roles by not investing any of her real emotions. She points out that she has never had to experience the things her characters go through, so she uses her imagination. And she has also (very sensibly) said that if at any point she felt that to improve her performance she had to lose a bit of her sanity, she would just stop, and do comedies instead.

"People expect me to be intense and dark . . . I'm not at all!"

This practical attitude would stand her in good stead. Jennifer was, after all, soon to take a role in a movie in which children were forced to kill one another. Probably best to only use her imagination!

Jennifer's Mystique

The Big Time

Jennifer's first starring role in a massively popular film franchise was not actually *The Hunger Games*, it was in the *X-Men* series. In 2011, she was cast as shape-shifter Raven Darkholme/Mystique in an *X-Men* prequel set in the 1960s, called *X-Men: First Class*.

This move from tortured indie movies to a giant blockbuster was all part of a well thought out plan. As Jennifer later explained to *Teen Vogue* magazine, when one thing gets really big, if you want to avoid being pigeonholed, it's good to then go and do the opposite.

London Life

The role required Jennifer to uproot to London while filming in Pinewood Studios. She lived in fashionable Notting Hill and hung out with her friend and *X-Men* co-star Zoe Kravitz, daughter of rock star Lenny Kravitz. 'I had a blast,' she told *Teen Vogue*. 'I was living in London for five months, and the whole cast . . . we got addicted to hanging out.' More importantly, she met the British actor Nicholas Hoult, who is now her boyfriend.

Did you know?

Jennifer now lives in Santa Monica, California, with her dog, a Yorkie.

Turning Blue

For about 10 per cent of the film time, Jennifer was onscreen as Mystique, which was just as well, given what getting made up for the role entailed. She had to have six layers of blue body paint, hand glued scales and yellow contact lenses! It could take up to eight hours to get her ready for the role. Jennifer took it in good grace and said that while she was being made up, she and the girls just giggled and watched films or *Sex and the City*. She couldn't even sit on a chair while being made up – she had to sit on a bicycle seat so that they could reach every bit of her!

Did you know?

She really can use a bow and arrow. For *The Hunger Games*, Jennifer trained with Olympic archer, Khatuna Lorig.

Hungry for The Hunger Games

It was in March 2011 that Jennifer, by now a big star, was offered the part of Katniss in *The Hunger Games*. She had already read the book and loved it, but even so, it took her three days before she said yes. The reason, unusually for Jennifer, was that she was scared of how big

Jennifer had to work out her fears

the movie would be. It was only her mother that made her see sense, pointing out to her that when she was doing indie movies rather than studio movies she'd always maintained that the size of the film didn't matter. So, knowing in her heart that she wanted to do this movie, Jennifer vowed not to let the opportunity pass her by just because it would be so huge. She just had to work out her fears.

Too Cool for Katniss?

When the casting was first announced, not everyone was pleased. Jennifer was too old to play Katniss, some people said, too pretty, not frail enough. But the makers of the film knew what they were doing and Jennifer did her bit to pacify the fans. Not exactly large at the best of times, she slimmed down even further and dyed her naturally blonde hair brunette. The proof was in the pudding – her Katniss has been universally greeted as a massive success.

Jennifer is a massive fan of Katniss and loves that every fan has a real relationship with her. She explained to *Teen Vogue* that Katniss is 'incredibly powerful, brave, and tough – and yet she has a tenderness and complexity.'

Josh Hutcherson

Name: Joshua Ryan Hutcherson
Birthday: 12th October 1992
Nickname: JHutch
Starsign: Libra
Height: 5'7"
Hometown: Union, Kentucky

Celebrity Teen

At the Start

Like Jennifer, Josh comes from Kentucky, and became an actor when he was still very young. He was already an established actor by the tender age of eleven, and says he'd wanted to be an entertainer since he was three years old. He loved watching actors on TV and always thought how cool it would be to be like them.

Home Sweet Home

There was nothing in Josh's background to suggest he was going to be such a precocious child. He attended New Haven Elementary School and his parents were childhood sweethearts. His father Chris is a management analyst for the U.S. Environment Protection Agency in Clifton and his mother Michelle used to work for Delta Air Lines as an emergency response trainer. When her son's career started taking off while he was still a little boy, she gave up her job to become his assistant. In 1996, Josh's little brother, Connor, came along and the family lived a comfortable suburban lifestyle, complete with two dogs and a swimming pool in the backyard.

Set on Acting

Initially, Josh's parents ignored their son's increasingly urgent wish to become a star. He would perform for the neighbours, singing and dancing away, but that was as far as it went to begin with, as both parents just hoped it would go away. But it didn't. Josh managed to get a part in a Kroger TV commercial and a Bible school training film – he was beginning to learn his trade. And so finally, after years of nagging, in January 2002 when Josh was still just nine, Michelle took him to an acting coach called Bob Luke at the Heyman Talent Agency in Oakley. Bob saw that Josh had a real talent and recommended that Michelle take him to Los Angeles for some auditions for television shows. And that was pretty much that.

> "Since I was three years old, I wanted to entertain people"

The Early Years

From that moment on, Josh and his mother effectively became commuters between LA and the family home in Kentucky, because Josh's career took off almost at once. He got a part in *House Blend*, a comedy pilot with Amy Yasbeck, followed by an *Animal Planet* movie called *Miracle Dogs* in which he was the lead, and then roles in *ER* and Lifetime's *The Division*.

Did you know?

If he wasn't an actor, Josh would love to be a football player.

Making Movies

It wasn't long before more films beckoned. Though not yet in his teens, Josh starred opposite the late Peter Falk and Timothy Daly in a made-for-television film *Wilder Days*, and also had a short role in the independent film *American Splendour*. There was also a small role in the Tom Hanks vehicle *The Polar Express*, a motion capture movie.

Hitting the Big Time

Josh's parents, though, wanted to keep his feet on the ground. When he was back in Kentucky, he was treated just like a normal kid, expected to do his chores and behave himself. Although money was now coming in, Josh was not allowed to fritter it away – in the course of eighteen months, he was allowed to buy a dirt bike, a laptop and a gas powered motor scooter which, it should be said, were things owned by most of the children who lived in the area.

Josh was now on the verge of real fame. It came as a shock to him the first time he saw himself on a billboard and he just started screaming! His mum was really affected too, and started crying. She'd never imagined that one day her son would be on a billboard on Sunset Boulevard in the middle of Hollywood!

Welcome to Hollywood

Hello Hollywood

By now, Josh was rarely out of work. Hollywood welcomed him with open arms, casting him in the Will Ferrell comedy *Kicking and Screaming*, as the voice of Markl in the animation *Howl's Moving Castle* and then as Gabe, the lead role in *Little Manhattan*, a film about pre-teen love.

Now thirteen, Josh was beginning to stand out. His next role was as Danny in the science fiction film *Zathura*. A year later, he played Robin Williams' son Carl, an adolescent weight lifter in the comedy *Runaway Vacation*. He followed this by playing Jesse Aarons in *Bridge to Terabithia*, about two ten-year olds (Josh could still just about get away with that!) who create a fantasy world called *Terabithia*.

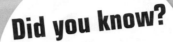

Did you know?

Josh got a turtle from Kristen Stewart for his 13th birthday.

Rising Star

Josh was also beginning to win awards. He won the Best Performance in a Feature Film – Leading Young Actor in the 2005 Young Artist Awards for *Zathura*, something he won again for *Terabithia*. Despite this rise to stardom, Josh could still live a relatively normal life, hanging out at the mall and eating his favourite ice cream. But things were changing. When out bowling one night, a little girl asked him to autograph a magazine which had a feature on him. Josh was beginning to turn into a heartthrob, although he was still a little shy about it back then.

Josh's next film to come out was *Firehouse Dog*, in which he played Shane Fahey, a fireman's son who befriends a dog. But he was growing up now and could no longer take the role of a small child. His films were becoming more grown-up, too . . .

> "He was that good!"

Josh is All Right

For someone who had been acting since the age of nine, it might be pushing it to call it a breakthrough role, but Josh got massive praise for playing Laser in the huge hit *The Kids Are All Right*, a film about a lesbian couple who have children through sperm donors. Josh won Breakthrough Actor in a Film at the Breakthrough of the Year Awards.

If he hadn't felt it already, Josh could now be sure – he really had arrived. It was after that film that it was announced that he'd landed the role of Peeta in *The Hunger Games* and was now set to become one of the biggest and hottest new stars of them all. *Hunger Games* author Suzanne Collins says Josh nailed his audition as Peeta. She says she would have cast him even if he had been bright purple and had six foot wings, they would have worked around the wings, "he was that good," Suzanne says.

The Next Big Thing

The next one, *Winged Creatures*, in which Josh played Jimmy Jasperson, involved victims of a shooting and how they dealt with the aftermath. It was 'very dark' according to one reviewer, although the critics were on the whole not very impressed. But Josh was mingling in pretty starry company now – co-stars included Kate Beckinsale, Dakota Fanning, Guy Pearce, Forest Whitaker and Jennifer Hudson. Not bad for a Kentucky teenager!

Josh's next role was as Sean, Brendan Fraser's nephew in *Journey to the Centre of the Earth*, which recieved fairly positive reviews. He then played Steve Leonard, one of two teenagers who broke a 100-year truce between two sets of vampires in *Cirque du Freak: The Vampire's Assistant*.

Did you know?

Josh celebrated getting the part of Peeta by going out for sushi.

The Future

Josh has said he will definitely stick with acting, but he'd also like to try directing one day. He already has a book he's keen on and might even try to write the screenplay himself, even if he needs someone to work with him on it.

Young Love

Did you know?

Josh's celebrity crush is Zoe Saldana, who starred in *Avatar*.

Star Dates

Josh's first serious girlfriend was the actress Shannon Wada, although he doesn't really talk about the relationship and they broke up around 2008. Since then, he's only had one really serious girlfriend, the actress Vanessa Hudgens, his co-star in *Journey2: The Mysterious Island,* who previously went out with Zac Efron.

The two were first spotted together in February 2011, and were then seen together the next month at a basketball game. They were a little coy about it at the time, but in January 2012, after they'd split up, they had to appear on a show to publicise the film. They were asked how long they'd been dating. 'We're not,' said Josh, after the two looked awkwardly at each other. Then he explained that they had been at some point, but now they were just good friends.

A Good Cause

After Josh had appeared in *The Kids Are All Right,* he became interested in the gay rights movement and became involved with the Straight, Not Narrow campaign, which encourages straight people to support their gay friends. He recorded a message for them, saying that it made sense for straight guys to support their gay friends – because it thins down the competition for the girls you like!

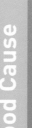

They were just good friends

A Regular Guy

But he's as normal as any other boy when it comes to the problems of dating. He was once asked about his most embarrassing moments and explained how when he was on a date he tried to put his arm around the girl. 'I was doing the yawn thing where you lift your arms up,' he explained. But it didn't go smoothly – as he did it he hit the table and knocked over a drink!

Liam Hemsworth

Name: Liam Hemsworth
Birthday: 13th January 1990
Nickname: Boo (But only Miley Cyrus uses it)
Starsign: Capricorn
Height: 6'3"
Hometown: Melbourne, Australia

An Aussie Upbringing

A Soapy Start

Unlike his two younger co-stars, both of whom came from Kentucky, Liam grew up on the other side of the world – Australia. In fact, Liam learned his trade in some of that country's most famous soap operas, including *Neighbours* and *Home and Away*, before relocating to the United States to pursue his career.

Brotherly Love

Liam was born in Melbourne, to Leonie, an English teacher, and Craig, a social services counsellor. Older brothers Luke and Chris are also actors and have appeared in Australian soaps – in fact, they sometimes go up for the same role! But the brothers are not jealous of one another. They have always been really close and Chris told *Movieline*, "It's not a spiteful, competitive kind of thing." Chris is six years older than Liam and Luke is nine years older.

Did you know?

Liam's brother told him he had to lose weight for *The Hunger Games*. His character is supposed to be starving!

First Girlfriend

Liam went to the local school and in Year Eight, he met Laura Griffin who, when he was fourteen, would become his first girlfriend. He and Laura were inseperable and Laura has said

He taught his first girlfriend to surf!

he was a bit of a joker, he taught her to surf and they would watch movies and go shopping together. In fact, they were together for five years, until Liam met Miley Cyrus.

Did you know?

Liam used to be a competitive surfer and made it to the state rounds where he competed with the top surfers in Victoria, Australia.

Boys Will Be Boys!

Liam's childhood was idyllic. When he was eight, the family moved to Phillip Island, and lived in a little beach town about two hours away from Melbourne, where he would spend his after school hours surfing with his brothers.

His big brothers also used him for target practice (in the nicest possible way), getting him to wear a couple of heavy sweaters and then prowling after him with air rifles. 'I feel like the worst brother in the world' Chris said, laughing. 'But he had a great time, OK!'

'I'd bend over to feed the guinea pigs and I'd get a pellet in the ass out of nowhere,' grumbled Liam. 'It really hurt.'

What Next?

When Liam left high school at sixteen, he wasn't really sure what he wanted to do. At first, he ended up laying floors for six months, for AU$15 an hour. But both his elder brothers were already acting and so Liam decided to follow in their footsteps.

He followed in his brothers' footsteps

When Chris had finished high school, his older brother Luke was on *Neighbours* and suggested he tried an acting course. Chris did, and it went from there. Liam followed the same path and did the same acting course after high school. And so the decision was made.

Soap Star

Big Break

It didn't take long for Liam to find his way. First he hired an agent, and then in 2007 started to land a couple of guest slots, in *Home and Away* (in which brother Chris had had a long running role as Kim Hyde) and *McLeod's Daughters*.

He then auditioned for *Neighbours* (where brother Luke had previously starred as Nathan Tyson) and landed the role of Josh Taylor, an athletic paraplegic who became involved in a relationship with the character Bridget Parker after she was paralysed down one side in a car crash. 'It could be pretty challenging,' Liam recalled. He tells a story of when the producer told him one day they'd have to cut around an entire scene because his leg was moving.

The producer had to cut around an entire scene because his leg was moving

Did you know?

Liam is considered one of the 55 faces of the future by *Nylon Magazine's* Young Hollywood Issue.

The Elephant Man

In 2008, Liam won the role of Marcus in *The Elephant Princess*, a children's show in which he played the very attractive lead guitarist in a band. Acting roles were coming in thick and fast now – he made a brief appearance in the short-lived television series *Satisfaction* and gained his first film role in the well-received psychological British-Australian horror film *Triangle*. Another followed, as a student in the Nicholas Cage vehicle, *Knowing*.

City of Angels

By this time, Liam and his brother Chris realised that if they wanted to have careers in the big league, then they were going to have to relocate to the centre of the action – Los Angeles! And so, in 2009, the two of them moved, first staying in the guest house of Chris's agent, William Ward, and then getting a place of their own.

Did you know?

Liam is very fit! He trains six days a week by surfing, lifting weights and boxing.

Healthy Competition

There followed a slightly complicated period in their lives, with the brothers going up for the same roles – although it didn't seem to do their relationship any harm. First, Liam was chosen to play a role in Sylvester Stallone's *The Expendables*, but the film was redrawn, with the part written out. He was gutted. Then he read for a role in the film *Thor* – but it eventually went to his brother Chris. However, that particular blow was blunted by the fact that he rapidly landed the part of Will Blakelee in *The Last Song*, where his love interest was to be pop star and teen sensation Miley Cyrus. Personally and professionally, Liam's life was about to undergo a huge change.

Life Imitating Art

The Last Song was about a troubled teenager, Veronica (played by Miley), reconnecting with her estranged father and falling in love with Liam's character Will at the same time. Reviews were rather mixed, but the film did well at the box office, propelling Liam into the spotlight and introducing him to Miley, with whom he formed an immediate bond. She was sixteen and he was nineteen. At first, the pair denied there was anything between them, but it soon became obvious they were more than just good friends.

Teen Winner!

As well as meeting Miley, Liam won many awards for his role in *The Last Song*, including Young Hollywood Breakthrough Of The Year at the Young Hollywood Awards 2010, Male Breakout at the Teen Choice Awards 2010 and Kids Choice: Fave Kiss at the Nickelodeon Australian Kids' Choice Awards 2010.

Liam's Girl

Chemistry with Cyrus

When Liam first met Miley, she wasn't sure what she felt about him – or what he felt about her. She wanted to concentrate on her work and didn't even think she wanted a boyfriend. But then the chemistry began to make itself felt . . .

Did you know?

Liam starred in the video for Miley's song 'When I Look At You'.

What a Gent!

Liam opened the door for Miley when they first met. No one had done that for her during her three years in LA! She told Ellen DeGeneres on the *Ellen Show* that Liam wasn't after the job of being her boyfriend, it's just that that was who he was. Miley was impressed. She turned to the director and said, 'He's got the job. He's hot and he opened the door. Excellent.'

> "OK, you're going to be my boyfriend!"

When they started working, together the chemistry was a bit awkward. They liked each other a bit, but it was difficult. So at one point Miley told him just to fake it and to pretend he liked her. When Liam said he didn't have to pretend Miley thought, 'OK, you're going to be my boyfriend. Cool.'

Ups and Downs

But the course of true love never does run smooth. The couple split up in August 2010, got back together again that September, split up again in November and by April 2011 were a couple once more. And as far as anyone knows, that is still how they are today!

A Charitable Boy

Liam knows how lucky he is, both in having had a loving childhood and in the success he's enjoyed, and so he wants to give something back. He is an ambassador for the Australian Childhood Foundation, which helps children who have been the victims of neglect, violence and abuse. Given what his parents did for a living, it was a cause very close to his heart.

'I have the best parents you can have,' he said when taking up the role. 'They have worked in child protection for twenty years and have only ever given me encouragement and support. The world is a scary enough place as it is for children. It is important that home should always be a safe place for them.'

> "I have the best parents you can have"

He is very modest. When he was asked if he was a hero to children, he said he didn't know, but he'd like to be, and he'd like to be a good role model.

Did you know?

Liam is very clean! 'I have incredible hygiene,' he told *Moviefone*. 'I have showers all the time I smell good!'

Liam On Screen

Competition!

Liam will be in all four films (like the *Harry Potter* series, the last book will be made into two films). He, Jennifer and Josh have all signed up for the entire run! But Liam wasn't the only guy to audition for the role of Gale. Selena Gomez's on-screen brother David Henrie also tried for the part. So did Nickelodeon's Alex Heartman.

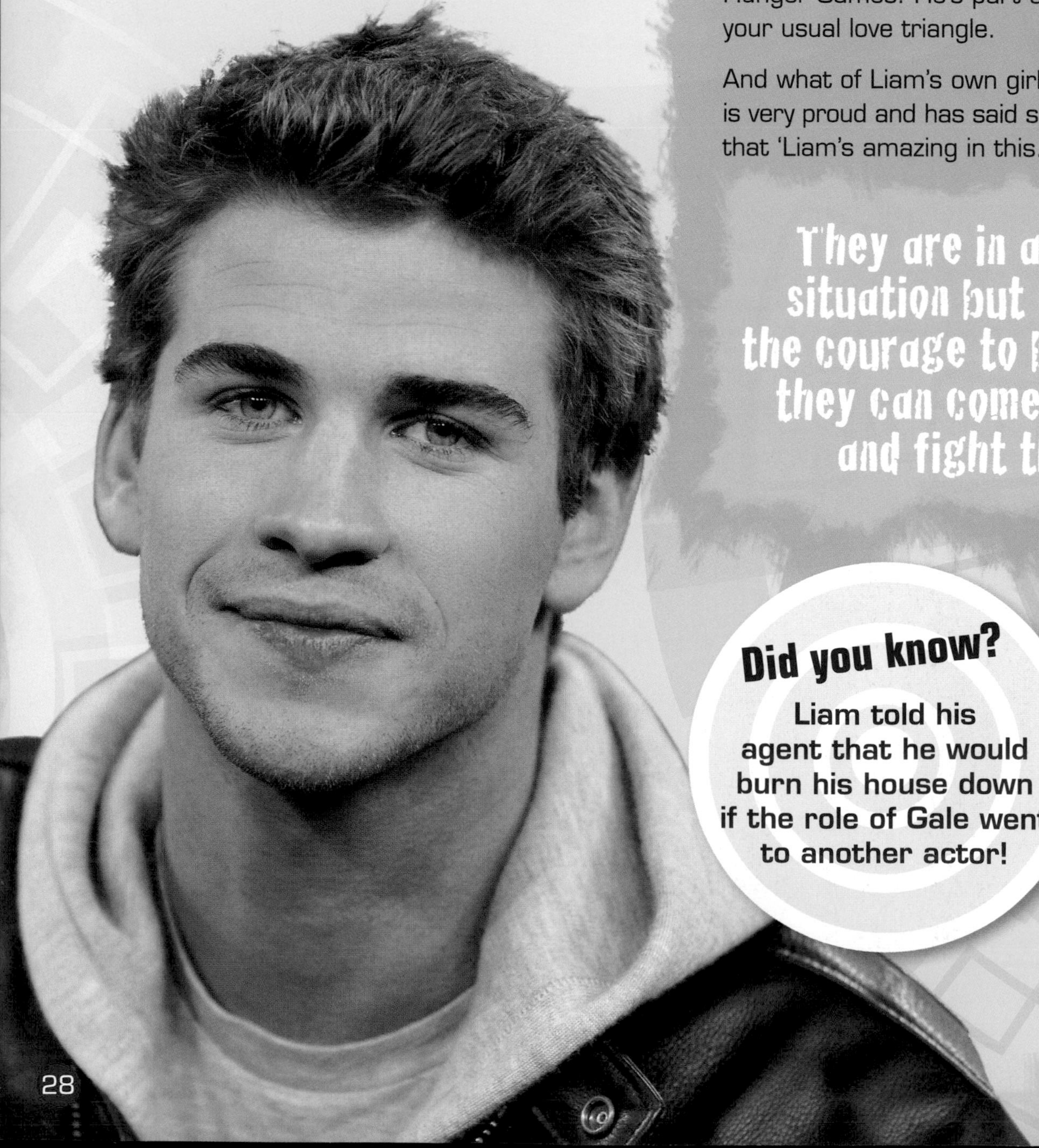

He's Fan-tastic!

Liam is a big fan of the Hunger Games books and loves the way that you really care about the strong characters. They are in a horrible situation but are given the courage to believe that they can come together and fight the evil. His character, Gale, is an extraordinary person who is very strong minded, and very against the Hunger Games. He's part of a love story, not your usual love triangle.

And what of Liam's own girlfriend? Well, Miley is very proud and has said she loves the film and that 'Liam's amazing in this.' We agree, Miley.

They are in a horrible situation but are given the courage to believe that they can come together and fight the evil

Did you know?

Liam told his agent that he would burn his house down if the role of Gale went to another actor!

Did you know?

Liam had to dye his hair brown for the film as he's a natural blonde. So did Jennifer. But brown-haired Josh had to go blonde!

Beauty Guide

Katniss Everdeen

Katniss is an outdoor girl with a fresh-faced, natural look. Learn how to capture her subtle, wild beauty with our make-up tutorial and be the feistiest girl this side of District 12!

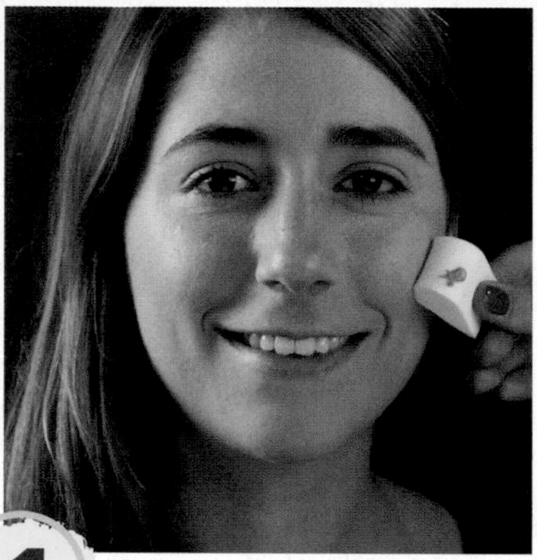

1 Create a light, dewy base by applying tinted moisturiser with a sponge, blending it into the neck and adding concealer if you need it.

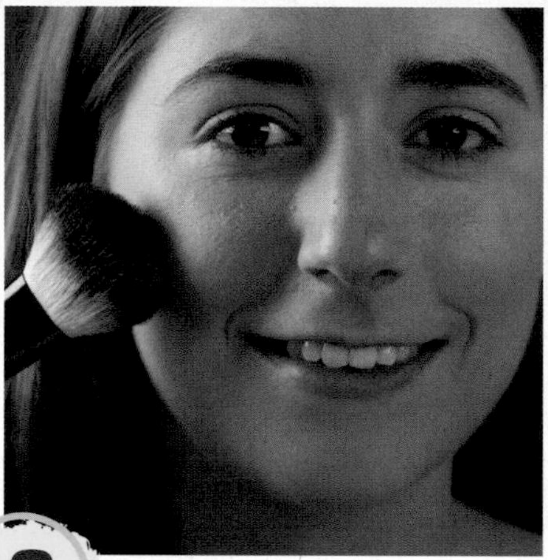

2 Add some peach or pale pink blusher to the apples of your cheeks and set the base with a dusting of loose powder.

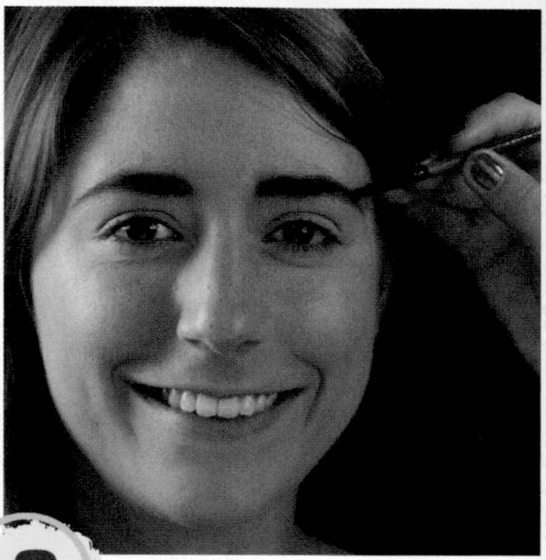

3 Finely fill in your brows with a small brush and an eyeshadow one shade darker than the hair. A defined brow really frames the eyes.

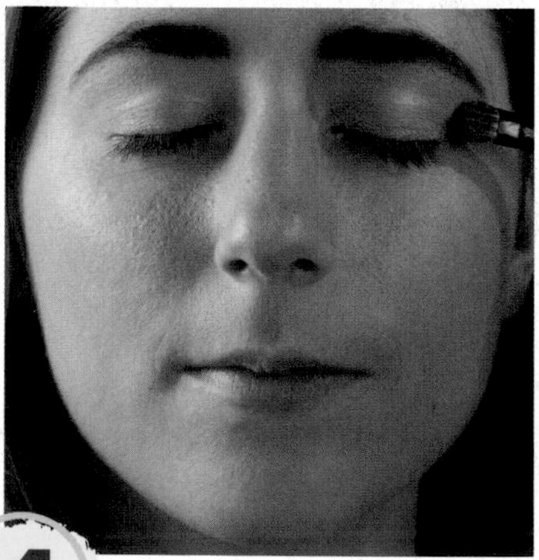

4 Take a nude eyeshadow, one shade darker than your eyelids. Close your eyes and brush it over the sockets.

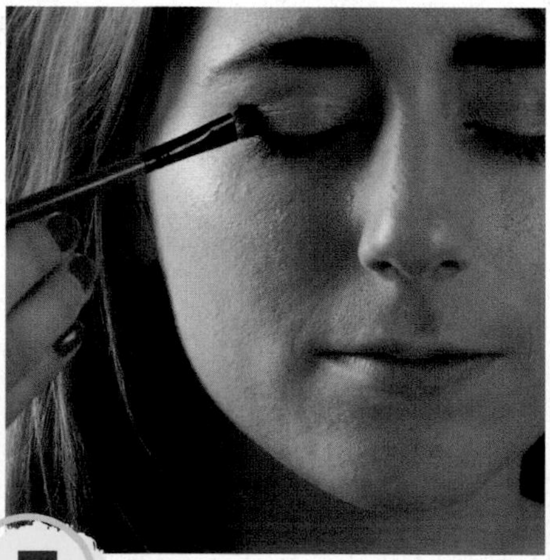

5 Now apply dark brown eye shadow into the crease of the eyelids, blending with a brush to create a smooth finish.

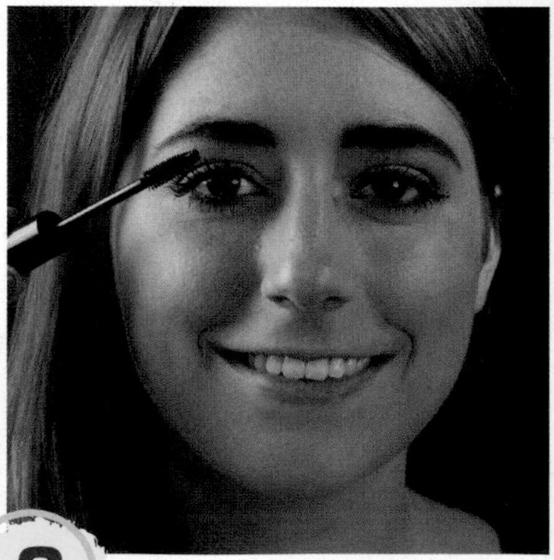

6 Use a soft brown kohl liner to smudge a fine line along the upper and lower lash lines then finish with black mascara and tinted lip balm.

Braidy Bunch

Don't forget the Katniss braid! First, create texture using curling tongs on a low setting. Then, plait a French braid from one side of your head to the other, letting it fall over one shoulder. Pull a few strands loose around the face to create a windswept look.

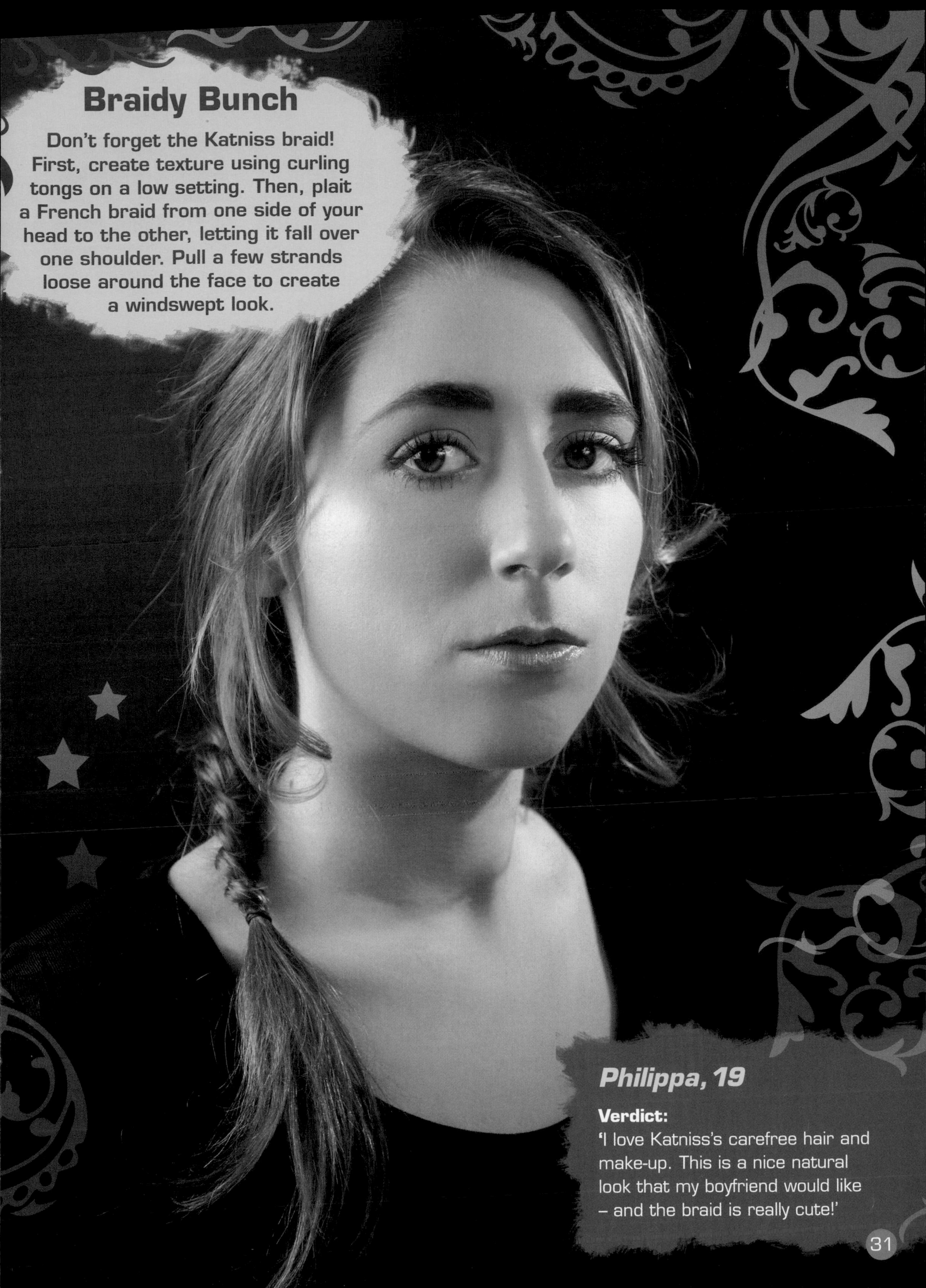

Philippa, 19

Verdict:
'I love Katniss's carefree hair and make-up. This is a nice natural look that my boyfriend would like – and the braid is really cute!'

Jennifer Lawrence

If you prefer Jennifer Lawrence's real-life style, we've got the hot tips to help you recreate it! Jen is a sun-kissed California beauty, who loves to accentuate her eyes with bronzed movie-star make-up.

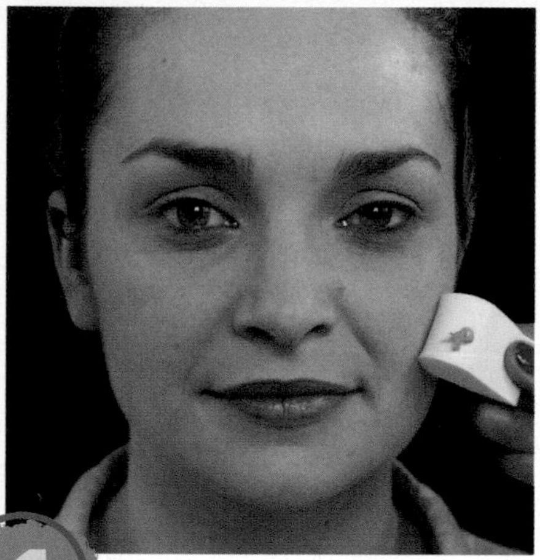

1 For a flawless finish, apply foundation with a sponge, blending into the neck. Use concealer under the eyes and on any blemishes.

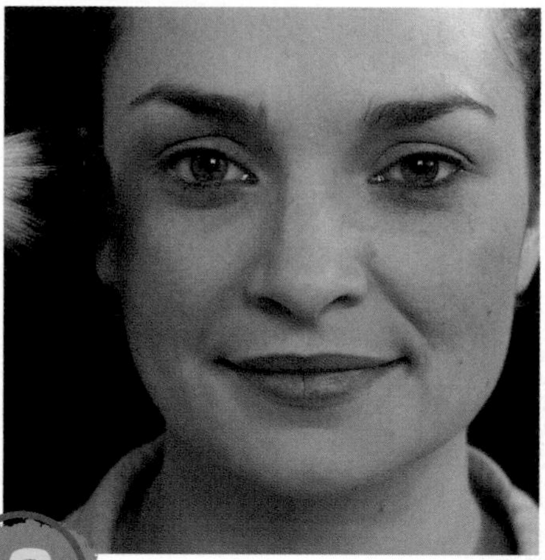

2 Set your face with loose powder, then add a natural glow to your cheekbones, nose, forehead and chin with a dusting of bronzer. Fake it, don't bake it!

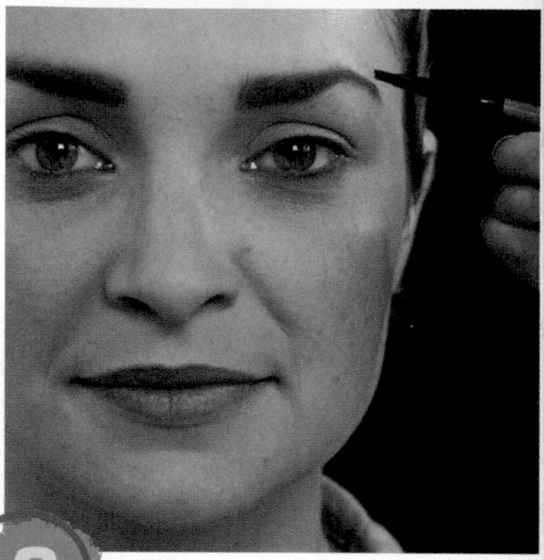

3 Fill in your brows using a small brush and a shadow one shade darker than your brow colour.

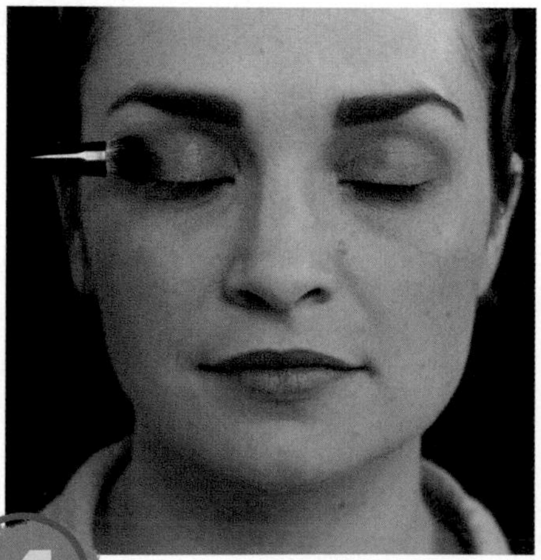

4 Apply a light copper eyeshadow over your entire eyelid, blending up towards your brows.

5 Brush a darker bronze shadow along the crease, then add a very dark brown shade at the outer corners of the eye, making sure to blend.

6 Line the upper and lower lash lines with black kohl pencil and smudge, then apply it to your inner lids, too. Finish with mascara and pale pink lipgloss.

Curl Girl

To copy Jennifer's cool tousled hairstyle, use tongs to create curls all over your head, then gently brush out and separate the curls with your fingers, finishing with a spritz of hairspray.

Jessica, 21

Verdict:
'I love the bronzed beachy feel of Jennifer's look, with a touch of Hollywood glamour. I'm definitely going to do my hair like this at home!'

Get the Look

Want to steal Katniss's look? Find out how to dress the part with our fab fashion guides!

Hunting

When Katniss goes hunting in the woods, she keeps it simple and practical to blend in with her environment with hardy fabrics like denim and cotton in earthy camouflage colours.

Chosen

Shine like Katniss when she volunteers, with a knee-length tea dress with a sash in pale blue cotton or denim. Pin your hair in two French braids to complete the look.

Urban Style

Mining Chic

Katniss and Peeta cause a sensation in their flaming black leather outfits. Get the look without the fire hazard using a fitted black leather jacket and braids pinned around your head.

Dress to Impress

For a more sophisticated look, try a girl-on-fire red dress and a winning smile. To recreate this look, go for bold red shades in simple, flowing shapes.

Are you a Natural Blonde

Jennifer's blonde, but she went many shades darker to play the role of Katniss. People say that blondes are bubbly and bright, while brunettes are bold and serious, but can it really be true that blondes and brunettes have different personality types? And does your personality go with your natural hair colour? Take our fun quiz to find out!

1

Is your favourite type of shoe:

a A strappy sandal

b Combat boots

Answer............

2

What breed of dog do you like best?

a Pomeranian

b Labrador

Answer............

3

You have a free afternoon. Do you:

a Go to the shopping mall and spend the day gossiping with your friends, trying on everything in Primark and looking out for cute guys while you drink Diet Cokes?

b Make a packed lunch, cycle to the nearest area of natural beauty and spend the day hiking in the hills with your friends?

Answer............

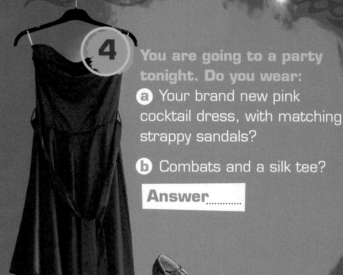

4

You are going to a party tonight. Do you wear:

a Your brand new pink cocktail dress, with matching strappy sandals?

b Combats and a silk tee?

Answer............

5

When you grow up you want to be:

a An actress, with a huge mansion in LA, a wardrobe to rival Victoria Beckham and a husband like Zac Efron?

b A vet with a large farmhouse in Yorkshire, a whole pack of dogs and a wardrobe of wellies?

Answer............

or Brunette?

6 **What's your favourite type of holiday?**

a) A beautiful hotel by the sea with white sandy beaches and plenty of opportunity to show off your bikini.

b) A wildlife adventure spotting gorillas in the jungle.

Answer............

Mainly As:
Congratulations, you're a beautiful blonde like Jennifer!

7 **How many lipsticks do you own?**

a) 12

b) 2

Answer............

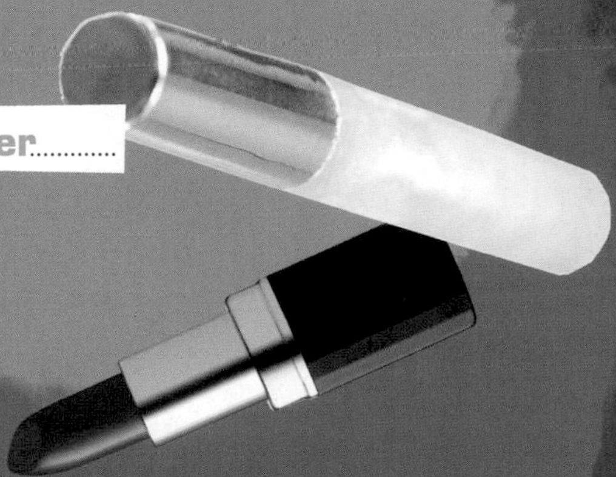

You lucky girl, you're a brilliant brunette like Katniss!

Team Peeta or Team Gale?

Katniss has got two hunky men competing for her affections – so which will she go for? Find out who is your perfect love match by answering the questions below.

1 Do you like the idea of a secret suitor?

a Yes

b No

Answer............

2 Is a big gesture important to you?

a Yes

b No

Answer............

3 Do you prefer a guy who is:

a Practical

b Idealistic

Answer............

4 Your ideal man is:

a Witty

b Sincere

Answer............

5 Your perfect date is:

a A big party

b A picnic in the countryside

Answer............

6 The most important part of a relationship is:

a Passion

b Friendship

Answer............

7 You like guys who are:

a Light hearted and funny

b Dedicated to a cause

Answer............

8 When you see your guy you feel:

a A little scared and excited

b Happy because you're such good friends

Answer............

9 Do you fall in love easily?

a No

b Yes

Answer............

10 Do you need a guy to be totally open, always?

a Yes

b No

Answer............

Now, how did you score?

Mainly As:

Yes, you're Team Peeta! You like the idea of a guy who's always held a torch for you and who is prepared to make a big gesture. You also like someone who can charm a crowd, raise a laugh and get people on his side. But don't forget romance. You love passionate gestures, and you like to feel your heart skip a beat when you're out on a date. And you like the feeling that you're always going to feel totally safe with your man.

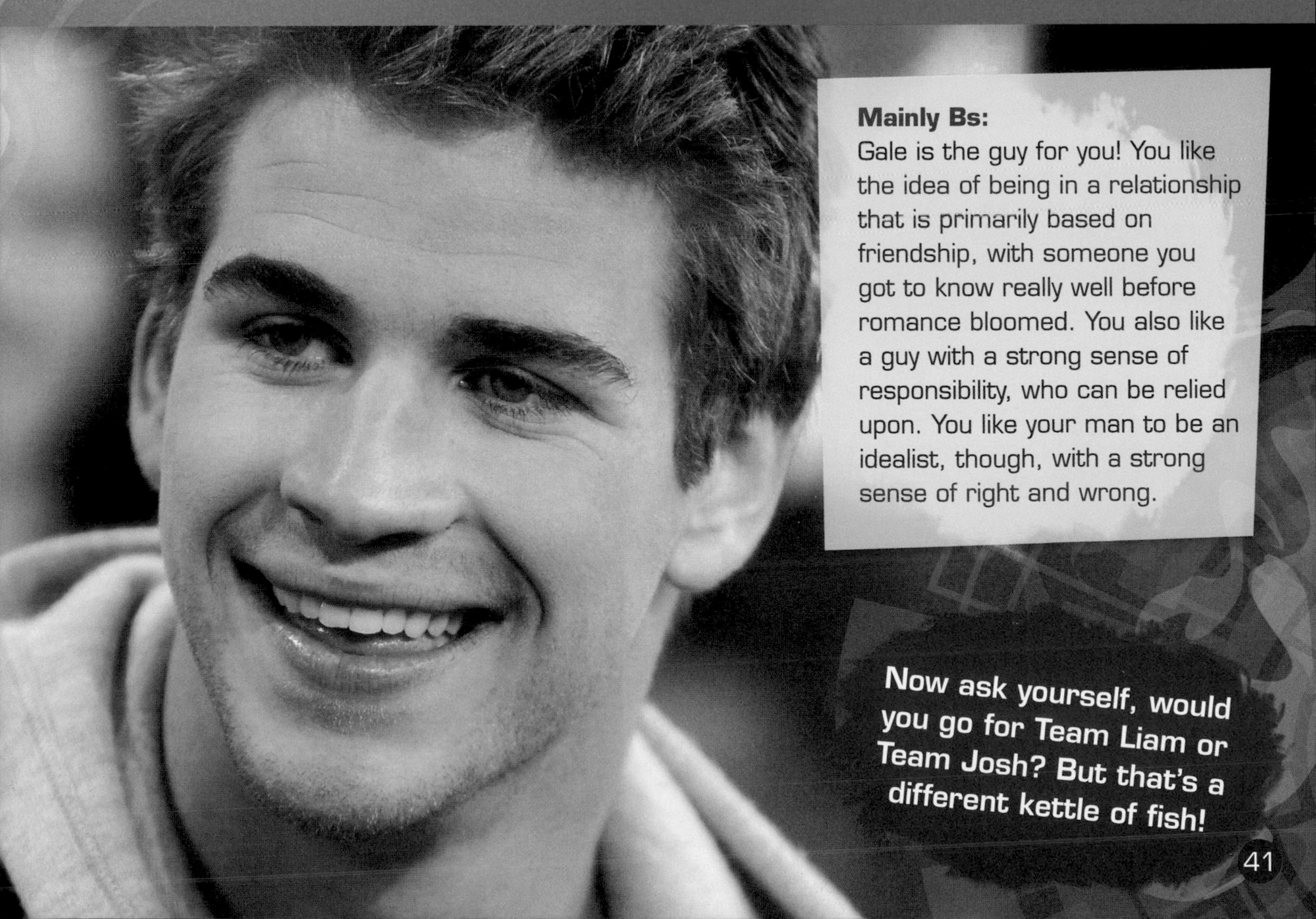

Mainly Bs:

Gale is the guy for you! You like the idea of being in a relationship that is primarily based on friendship, with someone you got to know really well before romance bloomed. You also like a guy with a strong sense of responsibility, who can be relied upon. You like your man to be an idealist, though, with a strong sense of right and wrong.

Now ask yourself, would you go for Team Liam or Team Josh? But that's a different kettle of fish!

Town vs Country: Where Do

The Hunger Games take place in Panem, a brutal post-apocalyptic society that lies in what was once North America. Its landscapes are very different, just like the places we all come from and want to live in can also be different. But would you prefer to live in the town or the country? Take our fun quiz to find out if you're a city slicker or a country bumpkin.

1 Your favourite TV programme is:

a *Made in Chelsea*

b *Countryfile*

Answer............

2 Is your most treasured possession:

a A beautiful necklace

b A mountain bike

Answer............

3 What best sums up your philosophy in life?

a Diamonds are a girl's best friend

b Red sky at night, shepherd's delight

Answer............

4 In your spare time you:

a Call all your best friends and arrange to spend the afternoon in the mall

b Go for a long healthy hike, followed by a barbecue back home

Answer............

5 Home is:

a A penthouse overlooking the cityscape

b Down on the farm

Answer............

6 Clothes are:

a A reason to get up in the morning

b Well, you'd be pretty cold without them, wouldn't you?

Answer............

7 If you're eating out, you like:

a A glamorous restaurant, filled with the top stars

b A rustic pub in the country, with the owner's dog asleep under the table

Answer............

You Belong?

8 **You buy your clothes from:**

a Top Shop

b Land's End

Answer............

9 **What's your favourite movie?**

a *Enchanted*

b *Cold Comfort Farm*

Answer............

10 **Your favourite flower is:**

a An orchid

b A daisy

Answer............

11 **What type of pet do you have?**

a A cat. They don't need looking after and they're elegant enough to match the surroundings. And you admire something so self-contained

b A dog. The two of you love taking long walks out together and you relate to an animal that likes the fresh air. And you love something so affectionate

Answer............

12 **Preparing for a day out at the beach you:**

a Have a self tan and a pedicure, buy a new bikini and stock up on sun tan lotion. You don't want to overdo it in the sun's bright rays!

b Bung your one piece and a few towels into the Land Rover

Answer............

13 **For your birthday, you want:**

a Something that sparkles, the more carats the better

b A horse

Answer............

14 **Your nails are:**

a Always perfectly manicured, with a soft neutral polish as it looks more sophisticated

b Broken with, if you're honest, a little grit underneath them . . .

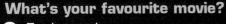

Answer............

15 **If the tyre on your bike deflated you'd:**

a Take it to a garage to be fixed

b Repair it

Answer............

16 **Cows are for:**

a Skinny lattes

b Clotted cream

Answer............

17 **What job do you want to do when you're older?**

a A booker in a model agency

b You've always secretly fancied driving a tractor

Answer............

18 **Grooming is:**

a An essential part of my beauty routine

b Something the horses need every day

Answer............

19 **Your favourite food is:**

a Sushi

b Venison pie

Answer............

20 **When you get married, the ceremony will be in:**

a St Paul's Cathedral, followed by a reception in a swish hotel

b The local village church, followed by a knees up at a country house

Answer............

21 **Fur is:**

a To be avoided now that such good quality reproductions are available (although it doesn't totally count if it's Granny's old fur stole)

b Something animals wear

Answer............

22 **You have a massage:**

a Once a month

b A what?

Answer............

23 **Your ideal car is:**

a A sports car, preferably a convertible

b A four wheel drive

Answer............

24 **Contemporary art is:**

a Visionary

b Squiggles

Answer............

Now tot up your score.

If you're mainly As – you're a townie, through and through. For you it's all about shopping, shopping and then some more shopping, and you put a lot of thought into the way you look. When you're not shopping, you're going to the movies or hanging out with your friends – sometimes a gang of you get together and practise beauty treatments and make-up lessons. But don't forget – there's a whole different world beyond the city limits you can sometimes escape to, too!

If you're mainly Bs – you're a real country bumpkin, never happier than in a pair of old jeans and some wellies, taking long walks through the fields or helping out on the farm. You love animals, especially dogs and horses, although you know that as well as pets, they serve a practical purpose and you should always treat them well. In the evenings, you're happier at a little local restaurant than a swish eaterie – but remember, the city's not all bad. There's plenty of culture to be found there, too!

Flora in the Wilderness

Jennifer, Josh and Liam had to get used to all sorts of weird and wonderful creatures in the post-apocalyptic wilderness of Panem, some lethal, others less so. For anyone to survive the Games it's necessary to know something about the plants and the strange mutated beasts that exist to haunt your every turn.

In the real world, plants can also be crucial to survival, either as food or for medicine. Here's a list of plants from around the world that would help you survive a spell in the wilderness. But remember, plants can be poisonous and even the good plants can have lookalikes that are poisonous, so you should never, ever eat anything from the wild unless you are with an expert who knows exactly what to look for.

Agave

These plants are found in hot countries and the desert and have a huge, fleshy stalk. You can cut into the stalk and drink the juice inside and you can also use fibres in the leaves for making ropes. The agave flowers only once before dying, the flowers and the bud can be eaten, although you should boil them first.

Cattails

These grow all over the world near water. However, never take them from contaminated water, because they will be contaminated, too. You can eat the young shoots raw or cooked and the pollen is a very good source of starch.

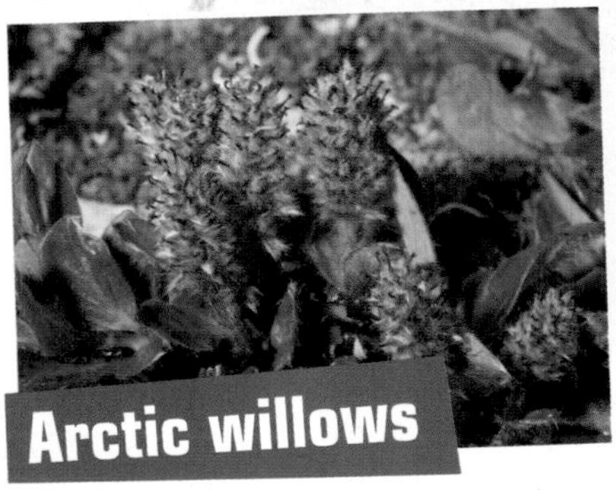

Arctic willows

Found in Europe, parts of the willow are edible. When new shoots appear, peel off the outer bark and eat the inside. It's a rich source of vitamin C.

Bamboo

Bamboo is found in Asia and the young shoots are edible, raw or cooked. However, they have a slightly bitter taste, which is removed by boiling. You can also use bamboo for numerous other things, including making a shelter, but young shoots can explode in a fire, so be careful!

Some types of cactus

Cacti may produce fruit, which is edible. The pulp, which is in the stem, also supplies water.

Nettles

Nettles have gained a lot in popularity in recent years, with many people using them in salads. The shoots and leaves are edible and extremely good for you, although you have to boil them for at least ten minutes to get rid of the sting.

And here are some plants that can act as medicine:

Aloe Vera

The leaves can be used to heal burns, wounds and other skin problems.

Dock leaves

If you get stung by the nettles, rub the area with a dock leaf (which conveniently is often growing nearby), which will act as a natural antihistamine.

Coca

This is found in South America. It used to be used as a local anaesthetic and people still drink coca tea for well-being and to ward off altitude sickness.

Elderberries

Not just a type of food, these have traditionally been used to treat pains, swellings, a range of infections, the flu and even the common cold.

Lavender

It was used as an antiseptic. It had other uses too – the Egyptians used it when they were mummifying bodies!

The Ultimate Fan Quiz!

Our stars know every detail of *The Hunger Games* world. Take our super fan quiz and find out if you can match their knowledge.

1. Woody Harrelson, who plays Haymitch Abernathy, became famous in a US sitcom in the 1980s. What was it called and what was the name of the character he played?

2. *The Hunger Games* is the first film since *Avatar* to remain top of the box office for a certain number of consecutive weeks. What is that number?

3. What is the name of the author of *The Hunger Games*?

4. What is the name of the President of Panem and who plays him in the film?

5. Jennifer Lawrence underwent a six week training scheme before she embarked on filming, including archery, rock and tree climbing, combat, running and yoga. On the last day of training she had an accident. What happened?

6. What actually happened to Alexander Ludwig?

10 In December 2011 a single from the film's soundtrack was released. What was it called and who sang it?

7 What did both Liam Hemsworth and Jennifer Lawrence have to do for their role in the film?

11 How many films are scheduled to be made based on the original trilogy of books?

12 Elizabeth Banks played the role Effie Trinket. Like Woody Harrelson, she made her name in a television series. What was it called?

8 What do Hailee Steinfeld, Abigail Breslin, Emma Roberts, Saoirse Ronan, Chloë Moretz, Jodelle Ferland, Lyndsy Fonseca, Emily Browning, Shailene Woodley and Kaya Scodelario all have in common?

13 What is the name of the director of *The Hunger Games*?

9 Most of *The Hunger Games* was filmed in one place. Where was it?

14 Danny Elfman was originally to compose the score of the film but had to leave due to a scheduling conflict. What is the name of the man who replaced him?

15 What do Alex Pettyfer, Lucas Till, Nico Tortorella, Alexander Ludwig, Evan Peters and Hunter Parrish have in common?

16 What was originally the total budget for the film and how much did it actually cost to make?

17 Four weeks before the film opened, film company Lionsgate began selling advance tickets and broke the one-day record held by another film. What was that film?

18 Elizabeth Banks had to undergo a lengthy grooming ritual every day on set. What was it?

19 Lenny Kravitz plays the roll of the stylist, Cinna. What is he best known for?

20 What was the film's working title before its release?

21 The film has been shown in many different countries with many different titles. What is the title in Spanish?

22 What do Chris Massoglia, David Henrie, Robbie Amell and Drew Roy all have in common?

23 What is the name of the actor who played Caesar Flickerman?

24 Jennifer Lawrence was originally scheduled to star in another film but dropped out to take part in *The Hunger Games*. What was it called?

Turn to page 60
to see how you did!

Hungry for Cake?

No celebratory banquet is complete without a variety of beautiful little cakes. Follow these instructions to create some stunning treats to wow your guests.

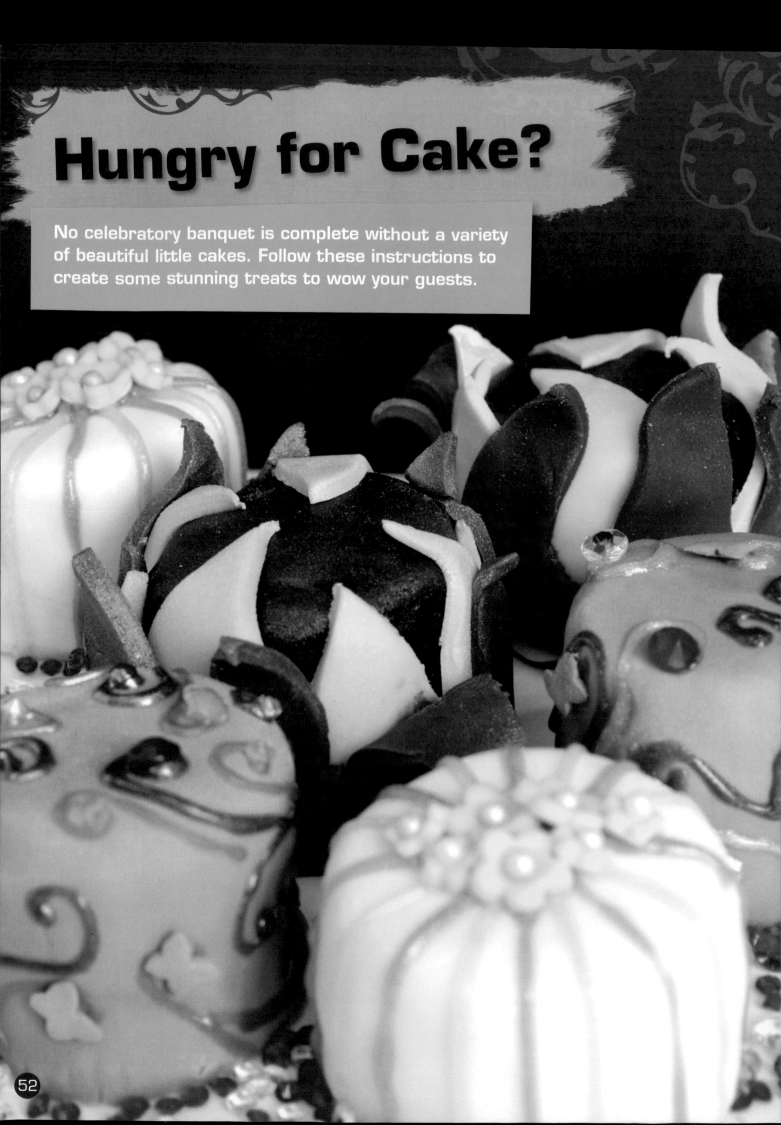

Creating and icing your cakes

Before you can start decorating your cakes you need to cover them with a layer of icing.

You will need:

To make six cakes

- 3 ready-made Madeira cakes
- A 3-inch fluted cutter
- A palette knife
- Vanilla butter icing
- 1kg ready-to-roll white icing
- Pink and black food colouring
- Rolling pin
- A sharp knife* (be careful!)

1 Use your fluted cutter to cut out six circular pieces from the Madeira cakes. Push them out gently and set to one side.

2 Using a palette knife, carefully cover your little cakes all over with butter icing, and leave to cool uncovered in a fridge for ten minutes. Now cut your ready-to-roll white icing into five pieces.

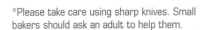

*Please take care using sharp knives. Small bakers should ask an adult to help them.

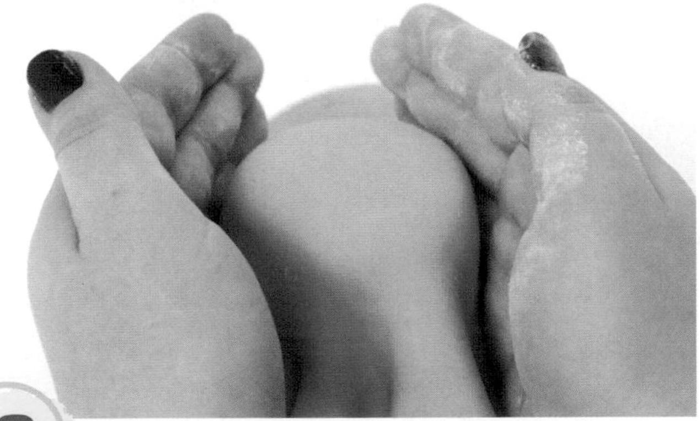

3 Take three pieces of the icing and colour one pink and one black. Leave the third piece white. Roll out your icing to about 3mm thick, then place over a cake. Smooth down the edges and use a knife* to cut away any excess icing around the bottom.

4 Follow the same steps to make two pink, two white and two black icing covered cakes. Now you're ready to decorate them! Turn the page for three delicious Hunger Games inspired styles . . .

Decorations

You will need:

- Purple, blue and pink gel icing tubes
- Yellow and red food colouring
- Flower cutters or knife*
- Sugar balls
- Edible silver and gold glitter spray
- Sugar or gel diamonds
- Sugar butterflies

Petite Primroses

Everyone will adore these dainty little treats. Some cultures believed that primoses were fairy flowers that could give you the power of invisibility!

1. Use your white iced cakes for this recipe. Starting from the top, carefully squeeze stripes down the side of the cake with the pink and blue gel icing. Do this all the way around the cake.

2. Colour one of the remaining pieces of icing yellow and roll it out to about 3mm thick. Using a flower cutter, make six flowers in different sizes. If you don't have a cutter you can use a knife.*

3. Place the primroses on top of the cake, sticking them on with some gel icing.

4. Pop a little coloured sugar ball into each flower with some gel icing. Add the finishing touches with edible silver glitter spray or edible silver glitter.

*Please take care using sharp knives. Small bakers should ask an adult to help them.

Cakes on Fire

Create some really fiery fancies. The flames symbolise life, truth and power.

1. Use your black iced cakes for this recipe. Colour the last bit of white icing red. (Use the rest of the yellow icing from the Petite Primroses cakes.) Roll each of them out so they're long enough to wrap around the edge of the cake.
2. Using a knife* carefully cut out a strip of flame shapes from both the yellow and red icing.
3. Dampen the bottom of the yellow strip of flames with water and carefully wrap this around the base of the cake.
4. Repeat with the red flames and wrap them around the yellow flames. Add a bit of sparkle with some edible gold spray or glitter to finish off the design.

Trinket's Treats

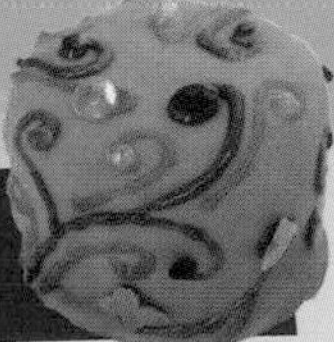

These little darlings make the perfect ornament to adorn any banqueting table.

1. Use your pink iced cakes for this recipe. Carefully make some sweet swirling patterns around the cakes with the gel icing tubes.
2. Now add your edible diamonds and butterflies to the cake. Use the gel to ensure they stick securely to the cake. You can make this as glittery and ornate as you want.

Inspirations!

Suzanne Collins, author of *The Hunger Games* trilogy, had many inspirations when writing the books, from Reality TV to Greek Myths. Here are some of them!

This is the Coliseum in Rome where gladitorial games took place thousands of years ago.

It's all a Blur

Suzanne has said that the idea for *The Hunger Games* came to her when she was watching television and kept switching channels between a reality show and news about Iraq. The two seemed to blur together, she said, as reality and violence mixed.

The Vietnam War

She was also influenced by the fact that her father fought in the Vietnam War when she was a child. He survived and returned home, but the sense of loss that she had was so great that she could empathise with Katniss's plight. Katniss lost her father when she was only eleven.

Gory Gladiators

But Suzanne had other inspirations, too. When the tributes are sent out to fight each other in the Arena, one obvious parallel is the gladiatorial games held by the Romans, in which warriors were sent out to fight each other, usually to the death.

Greek Myths

And there's an even more ancient inspiration for *The Hunger Games*. It is the story of one of the Greek myths – that of Theseus and the Minotaur. It goes like this . . .

Theseus and the Minotaur

Thousands of years ago, King Minos was competing with his brothers to rule Crete. To help his cause, he prayed to the sea god Poseidon to send him a white bull, which he would sacrifice.

Poseidon did so, but the bull was so handsome that Minos decided to keep it and sacrifice one of his own instead. The gods were angry about this, and in revenge made Minos's wife fall in love with the bull. As a result, the Minotaur, half man, half bull, was born. The Minotaur developed a taste for human flesh and was confined to a labyrinth in the palace, where he fed on Minos's enemies.

One day, King Minos waged a terrible war on the City of Athens. The Athenians were beaten, and begged King Minos for peace. He granted it, but only on the condition that every year they should send seven young men and seven girls to Crete to be devoured by the Minotaur.

On the third year, one of the seven young men was Theseus, son of the King of Athens. Like Katniss, Theseus volunteered. He was a great warrior and was determined to defeat the monster and stop this terrible practice. However, King Minos knew that even if Theseus managed to defeat the Minotaur, he would die anyway – he would never be able to find his way out of the labyrinth.

What Minos did not count on was that his daughter, Ariadne, would fall in love with Theseus. She decided to help him by giving him a role of thread which he could unravel on his way through the labryinth, and find his way out again.

Eventually Theseus came upon The Minotaur. He turned on him with a great roar and charged, but Theseus was unafraid. He fought bravely and slew the monster thus liberating his fellow Athenians and putting an end forever to the annual sacrifice. After that, he sailed back to Athens with Ariadne, whom he made his queen.

Did you know?

There are several versions of the myth. In one, the sacrifice takes place every *nine* years as revenge against Athenians for killing Minos's son

Putting it Together

Suzanne has often explained her Greek inspiration. The message from the Minotaur story is that if you mess with powerful people they will do something worse than kill you – they will go after your children. Parents sit by, powerless to stop it, until Theseus ends the reign of terror by killing the Minotaur. In Suzanne's story, Katniss is like a futuristic Theseus. But Suzanne hadn't wanted to use a labyrinth as her setting and chose instead to write an updated version of the Roman gladiator games.

Fun Facts

Read the books, seen the film? Now check out all these fantastic facts!

- Jennifer Lawrence and Paula Malcomson (Mrs Everdeen) have worked together before, playing mother and daughter in a 2003 episode of *Cold Case*.

- **Wes Bentley's very unusual beard that he sported for the role of Seneca was actually his own beard, not stuck on.**

- Elizabeth Banks' character's name is never mentioned in the film. It is Effie Trinket.

- **Jennifer accidentally kicked Josh in the head on set, knocking him unconscious. 'We were hanging out and she was like, "I can kick over your head" and I was like, "No way," ' Josh related. 'She said, "Watch!" But then she kicked me right in the temple. She felt so bad. She was crying.'**

- She hurt herself, too. When filming the last day of her six-week training phase, she ran full force at a wall but her foot gave out and she hit it full on. 'I had to get a CAT scan and go into a tube where they put this fiery liquid in your body.'

- ***The Hunger Games* smashed the box office record for most advanced tickets sold for opening day, which was originally held by *Twilight's Eclipse*.**

- Suzanne Collins, the author of the books, also wrote the script. It makes sense – her background is in playwriting.

★ **Most of the film was shot in North Carolina, around Asheville and Charlotte.**

★ This is the second film in two years in which Jennifer plays a part in which she catches and skins squirrels to feed her family. The first was *Winter's Bone.*

★ **When the book first came out, the print run was going to be 50,000 copies. This was almost immediately increased to 200,000. It has been translated into twenty-six different languages. Suzanne is also the first children's author to sell over one million Kindle eBooks and she is now the best selling Kindle author of all time.**

The Hunger Games have received numerous awards including:

- ★ ***Publisher's Weekly* Best Book of the Year for 2008**
- ★ ***The New York Times* Notable Children's Book of 2008**
- ★ **Gold Duck Award in the Young Adult Fiction Category 2009**
- ★ **2008 Cybil Winner for fantasy and science fiction books (along with Neil Gaiman's *The Graveyard Book*)**
- ★ **One of the *School Library Journal* Best Books of 2008**
- ★ **Booklist Editor's Choice 2008**
- ★ **California Your Reader Medal 2011**

Answers

The Ultimate Fan Quiz!

1. *Cheers* and Woody Boyd

2. Four

3. Suzanne Collins

4. President Coriolanus Snow, played by Donald Sutherland

5. She hit a wall running at full speed – but she was not badly hurt

6. He was cast in the role of Cato

7. Dye their blonde hair brown

8. They all auditioned for the role of Katniss

9. North Carolina

10. 'Safe & Sound' by Taylor Swift

11. Four

12. *30 Rock*

13. Gary Ross

14. James Newton Howard

15. They all auditioned to play Peeta Mellark

16. It was originally $88 million but cost $78 million – $10 million under budget!

17. *The Twilight Saga: Eclipse*

18. A 45 minute manicure

19. He is a singer-songwriter

20. Artemis

21. *Los Juegos del Hambre*

22. They were considered for the role of Gale

23. Stanley Tucci

24. Savages

How did you score?

0-5: Oh come on! Where have you been?

6-10: Could do better. Our stars would wipe the floor with you!

11-15: You're starting to show real fan potential.

16-20: Very impressive. You're not a clever cloggs from District 5 are you?

21-24: You certainly know your jabberjays from your mockingbirds! You've aced the Ultimate Fan Quiz!